essence of BLUE

Hilary Mandleberg

e s s e n c e   o f   BLUE

William Morrow and Company, Inc.

New York

Designer   Luis Peral-Aranda
Location Research   Nadine Bazar and Kate Brunt
Production   Patricia Harrington
Head of Design   Gabriella Le Grazie
Publishing Director   Anne Ryland

Library of Congress Cataloging-in-Publication Data

Mandleberg, Hilary.
Essence of blue / by Hilary Mandleberg.
p. cm.
ISBN 0-688-17431-0
1. Color in interior decoration.   I. Title.
NK2115.5.C6M36 2000
747'.94—dc21   99-36730
                                CIP

Printed and bound in China by Toppan Printing Co.
First Edition
10 9 8 7 6 5 4 3 2 1
www.williammorrow.com

contents

shades of blue

Blue is said to be the favorite color of most people. Could this be because it puts us closer in touch with nature, reminding us of the sea, the sky, and distant mountains? Is it because it helps to calm us and soothe away our worries? Different shades of blue can

STAIRWAY TO HEAVEN

have different effects. Light blue aids clear, creative thought, while deeper shades can convey a sense of dignity. Dark blues such as indigo may even induce a hypnotic effect. Enjoy blue's varied moods in each of your rooms, with paint, furniture, and accessories.

combinations

One feature of the color blue that makes it so very appealing for home decoration is the way that it combines

well with other colors. Some of these pairings are classics; you can always be sure they will look good. Blue with white is the first that comes to mind. This combination was used for many hundreds of years by the Chinese for

their porcelain; it inspired the Dutch to make their famous blue and white china in Delft. Distinctive blue and

There is no blue without yellow
Vincent van Gogh

white ceramic ware was produced in Portugal and Spain as well as in Iznik in Ottoman Turkey. When it comes to

choosing other combinations you can always look to an artist—and who better than Monet or Van Gogh, two of the greats? Monet was so enamored of blue and yellow that he chose to paint his own dining room in this irresistible

color combination. And note how blue of any shade looks regal with gold. Just a touch of gold makes the look work.

living/dining

Blue is relaxing and easy to live with. It also suits many decorating styles so is an ideal choice for living and dining rooms. And in case that were not enough, blue also has a spiritual dimension. In Chinese culture, blue represents immortality; in Buddhist

SINGING THE BLUES

art, wisdom and awareness are both depicted as bright blue. In your living and dining areas you can combine different shades of blue to strengthen the impact. But to prevent blandness from setting in, you should vary the patterns and textures. A mix of wood,

wicker and plaster painted in several
shades of blue looks charming; to jazz
up this look, add a burst of blue and

white gingham or ticking, or a flash
of contrast with a different color. This
could be something as basic as a red

stripe in a simple tablecloth or a bowl of green apples. Blue also makes the perfect foil for natural wood. Keep pale

wood looking cool and fresh with light
blue details; add to the richness of
dark wood with dusky shades of blue.

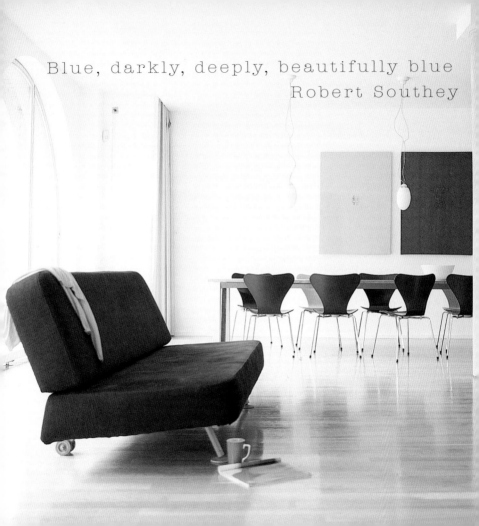

Blue, darkly, deeply, beautifully blue
Robert Southey

Large light-blue spaces with minimal furniture evoke a gentle mood of meditative calm, where you can observe the very essence of your being. So be sure and keep this room clutter free. Just add deep rich blue for extra drama.

kitchen

According to the world of color theory, kitchen colors should stimulate the senses and help you let go of the accumulated stresses of the day. Blues convey a sense of space and coolness, but they can sometimes be quite cold and frosty, especially in a kitchen,

COOKING BLUES

where creativity needs to be nurtured and family and friends made welcome. So temper your blues with the natural warmth of wood, terra cotta, wicker, and rope in order to create a relaxed, comfortable and friendly setting for inspired cooking and delicious meals.

Blue with stainless steel, shiny tiles and laminates, and molded plywood is stylish and contemporary. For a more

lived-in look, combine blue with old wood and a cozy assortment of much-loved cookware and great accessories.

bedroom

What could be more restful than the sound of waves gently lapping at the sides of a boat, or more serene than the sight of a clear blue sky hovering above a still blue sea? Blue is a color that recedes, conjuring up a sense of space and peacefulness, so is the ideal choice

AT THE SEASHORE

for relaxing bedrooms. Choose a blue and white striped cotton curtain to filter sunlight onto softly faded blue-painted furniture and create a languid sunbleached seashore mood. A child's sailor blouse brings back memories of days spent digging clams by the sea.

There is no need for morning blues if
you are lucky enough to wake up each
day in a bedroom imbued with a sense

of the country. It's easy to create this
feeling of rural warmth with polished
wooden floorboards and plenty of old

wooden furniture from junk shops and flea markets. Textiles can really come into their own in country bedrooms. For that homespun look, try a wide array of quilting, patchwork, gingham, lace, ticking, old well-worn blankets, softly faded flowery throws, woven runners, and rag rugs. A four-poster bed plump with down-filled bedding and enveloped in the thickest quilted fabric is the ultimate in country coziness. Or you could adapt the rural look for urban lifestyles by painting country wood or wicker furniture in white or shades of blue and gray. For a modern take on the traditional four-poster, just drape a simple bed frame with blue and white deck-chair fabric.

bathroom

Your bathroom is your sanctuary, the place where you can withdraw from the world and unwind to your heart's content. Bathe in blue and no matter where you are or what the season, you can imagine yourself in a calm blue lagoon or afloat in the wide blue

ALL WASHED UP

sea without a care in the world. With such a huge range of blues to choose from, there is sure to be one that is perfect for the mood you want to create. Choose light, cool blues to help you feel calm and removed from bustle and activity. What could be better after a stress-filled day at the office? Or perhaps you are attracted to the many possibilities of turquoise.

This green-tinted blue will guarantee refreshment for hot and aching limbs after a workout, or after hours spent

pounding the city sidewalks. Bathroom
blues come in many forms. Use shades
of blue for your paintwork or tiling—

those tiny mosaic tiles are great for
creating a dazzling image of brightly
sundrenched swimming pools. And now

add your choice of blue accessories—
soap dishes, shower curtains, towels
and soaps, bottles and jars. And with

blue curtains or blinds filtering the
light at the window, you can create
your very own cool, shady blue grotto.

outside

Blueness doth express trueness

Ben Jonson

Every color that is in the artist's or interior decorator's palette has its counterpart in the natural landscape, and nowhere is this more apparent than in the case of blue. Everyone thinks of the sky as blue, even when it is more of a gray color. But blue in

WIDE BLUE YONDER

nature does not stop with the sky. It is also the color of oceans and lakes, of distant mountains and of a large number of exquisite flowers. So when your choice is blue for decorating outdoors, you cannot fail to create a harmonious and pleasing impression.

Bright, clear blues are just right for the great outdoors. They conjure up a feeling of fun, holidays, the seaside,

beach shacks, endless sunshine, and tooling around in boats. Blue-painted old cane furniture, blue-washed wooden tables and chairs, modern blue plastic tableware, blue and white stripes and gingham are gorgeous in the garden,

stunning at the seaside, beautiful on boats and perfect for picnics. The look is relaxed, jaunty and totally fuss-free.

credits

Architects and designers whose work is featured in this book:

Key: **a**=above, **b**=below, **l**=left, **r**=right, **t**=telephone, **f**=fax

Ash Sakula Architects

38 Mount Pleasant

London WC1X 0AN

England

t 00 44 (0)20 7837 9735

Page 30

Barefoot Elegance

Dot Spikings & Jennifer Castle

Interior Designers

3537 Old Conejo Road

Suite 105

Newbury Park, CA91320

t 00 1 805 499 5959

Pages 54, 62-63

Nancy Braithwaite Interiors

2300 Peachtree Road

Suite C101

Atlanta, GA 30309

Page 50

Conner Prairie Museum

134000 Alisonville Road

Fishers, IN 46038

Page 33

Chris Cowper

Cowper Griffith Associates

Chartered Architects

15 High Street

Whittlesford

Cambridge CB2 4LT

England

Pages 8, 24-25, 38

DAD Associates

112-116 Old Steet

London EC1V 9BD

England

t 00 44 (0)20 7336 6488

Page 49 r

Ecomusée de la Grande Lande

Marquèze

40630 Sabres

Bordeaux

France

Page 42

Alastair Hendy

London-based food writer, art director

and designer

f 00 44 (0)20 7739 6040

Pages 46, 48 l

Hudson Featherstone Architects

49-59 Old Street

London EC1V 9HX

England

t 00 44 (0)20 7490 5656

Pages 29, 35 br

photographers

Front cover main Pia Tryde; **Front cover inset** Henry Bourne; **Back cover** Pia Tryde; **Spine** Henry Bourne; **Front flap** Tom Leighton/Siobhan Squire & Gavin Lyndsey's loft in London designed by Will White; **Back flap** Tom Leighton/a house in London designed by Charles Rutherfoord, bowl by Sue Paraskeva; **1** Tom Leighton/bowl by Sue Paraskeva; **2** Tom Leighton/a house in London designed by Charles Rutherfoord, bowl by Sue Paraskeva; **3** James Merrell; **4–5** Tom Leighton/Siobhan Squire & Gavin Lyndsey's loft in London designed by Will White; **6** Pia Tryde; **7 l** Henry Bourne; **7 r** Pia Tryde; **8** Simon Upton/a house in Cambridge designed by Cowper Griffths Associates; **9** Henry Bourne; **10** Simon Upton; **11 al & bl** David Loftus; **11 ar** Tom Leighton; **11 br** Tom Leighton/bowl by Sue Paraskeva; **12** James Merrell; **13 l & r** James Merrell; **14 l** Simon Upton; **14 r** Simon Upton/a house in Texas designed by Jacomin Interior Design; **15 l** David Loftus; **15 r** Simon Upton; **16–17** James Merrell; **18** Simon Upton/Lena Proudlock's house in Gloucestershire; **19** James Merrell; **20** Simon Upton; **21 l** Henry Bourne; **21 r** David Loftus; **22 al** Henry Bourne; **22 bl & r** James Merrell; **24 l** Henry Bourne; **24–25** Simon Upton/a house in Cambridge designed by Cowper Griffths Associates; **25** Tom Leighton/Roger Oates & Fay Morgan's house in Herefordshire; **26–27** Simon Upton/Lena Proudlock's house in Gloucestershire; **27** James Merrell; **28–29** Tom Leighton/Siobhan Squire & Gavin Lyndsey's loft in London designed by Will White; **29** Henry Bourne/a house in Devon designed by Hudson Featherstone Architects; **30** Henry Bourne/a house in London designed by Ash Sakula Architects; **31 l &** James Merrell; **32** Simon Upton/a house in Portugal designed by Vera Iachia; **33** Simon Upton/Conner Prairie Museum; **34** Ray Main/Malin Iovino's apartmen in London; **35 al** Simon Upton/a house designed by Maximilian Lyons; **35 ar & bl** James Merrell; **35 br** Henry Bourne/Dan & Claire Thorne's town house designed by Hudson Featherstone; **36** Tom Leighton; **37** James Merrell; **38** Simon Upton/a house in Cambridge designed by Cowper Griffths Associates; **39 l & r** James Merrell; **41** Henry Bourne; **42** James Merrell/Ecomusée de la Grande Lande; **42–43** James Merrell; **43** Tom Leighton; **44** Simon Upton/Lena Proudlock's house in Gloucestershire; **45** Simon Upton; **46** Andrew Wood/Alastair Hendy & John Clinch's apartment in London designed by Alastair Hendy; **47 l & r** David Montgomery; **48 l** Andrew Wood/Alastair Hendy & John Clinch's apartment in London designed by Alastair Hendy; **48 r & 49 l** Andrew Wood/an apartment in London designed by Littman Goddard Hogarth Architects; **49 r** Henry Bourne/bathroom by James Lynch of D.A.D. Associates; **50** Simon Upton/a house designed by Nancy Braithwaite Interiors; **51** David Montgomery; **52 l** Henry Bourne; **52 r** Tom Leighton; **53** Simon Upton/a house in Portugal designed by Vera Iachia; **54** Simon Upton/a house designed by Barefoot Elegance; **55 l** James Merrell; **55 r** Pia Tryde; **56 a & b** Pia Tryde **56–57** Simon Upton/a house in Portugal designed by Vera Iachia; **59 al & br** James Merrell; **59 ar & bl** Pia Tryde; **60 l** Simon Upton; **60 r** Pia Tryde; **61 l & r** Pia Tryde; **62–63** Simon Upton/a house designed by Barefoot Elegance; **64** Pia Tryde; endpapers Simon Upton/a house designed by Jacomini Interior Design

The author and publisher would also like to thank all those whose homes or work are featured in this book.